W9-CFM-531

MARK'S STORY
An Introduction to the Gospel of Mark

Gospel Storyteller Series

By Dr. Marvin G. Baker

Illustrated by Paul S. Trittin

innovative
Christian Publications

Copyright © 2003 by Dr. Marvin G. Baker

Mark's Story, An Introduction to the Gospel of Mark
by Dr. Marvin G. Baker
Illustrated by Paul S. Trittin

Printed in the United States of America

Library of Congress Control Number: 2003107802
ISBN: 0-9729256-0-0

All rights reserved. No part of this publication may be
reproduced or transmitted in any form or by any means
without written permission of the publisher.

Innovative Christian Publications
(a Division of Baker Trittin Concepts)
Grand Haven, Michigan

http://www.gospelstoryteller.com

Dedication

❧

This book is dedicated to the memory of my daughter, Evangeline (Vangie) Ruth Coleson (1949-2001). In 1995 Vangie asked, "What if the New Testament were transliterated in a style and reading level that children could easily read and clearly understand?" Based on that vision, *The Gospel Storyteller Series* is becoming a reality, and *Mark's Story, An Introduction to the Gospel of Mark*, is the first tangible evidence.

The Storyteller

Hello!

My name is John Mark. John's my Jewish name. Mark is the name the Romans gave me.

I have always wanted to tell my story. I guess that's really not so unusual. Many people have stories they want to tell. Growing older has given me time to think about the things that happened during my lifetime. Believe me, it takes time to realize how many of your dreams really did come true.

Through the years I met some wonderful people and have great memories! And I have an exciting story to tell you. Get comfortable. Relax. As you read my story, pretend I'm right there with you.

I lived during a most exciting time in history. All calendars are set from this time. The events that happened before the birth of my friend are written B.C. The things that happened afterward are written A.D. All dates are counted by beginning with the year he was born.

The things that happened in the country where I lived have made a difference in the history of the entire world. Many people don't know very much about the land where these events took place, so I'll share a few details as we go along.

This is my story about my friend, Jesus. The events are all true. The places are real. Picture the action clearly in your mind. In fact, picture what it would be like if it were happening in your own neighborhood today.

Fondly,

Mark

Chapter 1

❧

In the Old Jewish Bible, a man named Isaiah wrote about the Messiah, God's son, coming to earth. He also wrote that God would send someone to help people get ready to welcome His son. John the Baptist was the man God would send to do this.

My story begins over six hundred years later when I was just a boy living in the city of Jerusalem. This was several years after John the Baptist had been born. I was just a kid like you when all this happened.

John was an unusual man and some of the kids who had seen him thought he was a little strange. He wore really messy clothes made of camel's hair, and he held them together with only a leather strap.

For some reason he lived way out in the desert wilderness towards the Kingdom of Perea. Out there in the wilderness there was no place to buy food. That didn't really matter since he didn't have any money anyway. So he caught and ate grasshoppers. He also ate any wild honey he could find in the old hollow trees.

Perea was hilly country on the eastside of the Jordan River down near the Dead Sea. The Dead Sea is the lowest place on the surface of the earth and it gets really hot there. On the other side of the Jordan River was the Kingdom of Judea and over the mountains the beautiful city of Jerusalem.

In those days both Perea and Judea were parts of the Roman Empire. The Roman Empire was the most powerful government the world had ever known.

While he was living in the wilderness, John began to help people get ready for God's son. He often came down into the Jordan River valley to tell the people there about God's love.

If they confessed their sins to God, John baptized them. To do this he covered them with water from the Jordan River. People were baptized to let everyone know they loved God and were sorry for their sins.

People living in the Kingdom of Judea and up in the city of Jerusalem came down to hear John speak. It was not an easy trip. They had to walk miles down the rugged mountainside to

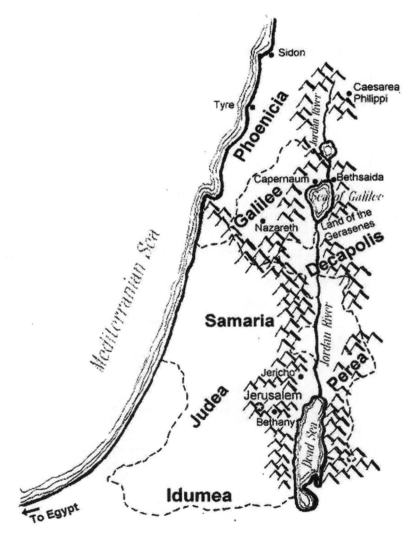

reach the Jordan River. Then afterwards they had to walk all the way back to the city. Lots of times John told them things they didn't want to hear. What he said made some people very angry, but the people kept coming.

John was well known for miles around. Even the people way up in the Kingdom of Galilee had heard of him. That was a long way from where John lived.

John's job was to tell people that a very important person was coming. He knew this man was better than he was. In fact, John said, "This man is so much better than I am that I'm not even good enough to untie this man's shoes. You all know that I use water to baptize people. This person who is coming will baptize people with the Spirit of God."

One hot day a man named Jesus came to the Jordan River where John was talking to the people. He had traveled from

the village of Nazareth. Nazareth was in the Kingdom of Galilee just a few miles from the Sea of Galilee. This was about 80 miles from where John preached. Without any roads it took several days to walk this far. The trail most people followed was very difficult. To make the trip even worse it could get extremely warm. Sometimes it got hotter down there in the valley than it was for miles around.

I don't know for sure which way Jesus took. The easiest one would be along the Jordan River. From his home in Nazareth he probably walked over the mountains to the Jordan River. Then he would walk all the way to the south end of the river.

When Jesus arrived where John was talking, Jesus said to him, "John, I want you to baptize me." John was not expecting this at all.

"I've been telling the people that I'm not worthy to untie your shoes," John replied. "Just imagine what they'll think if I baptize you!" With that, John tried to change the subject. But Jesus insisted that John do what he asked. John finally agreed and he baptized Jesus in the Jordan River just like he had baptized the others.

But at this baptism things were really different. When Jesus came out of the water, the skies opened. The Spirit of God came down like a dove and landed on his shoulder.

This was really unusual for doves are afraid of people. What was especially scary happened next. Everyone heard a voice coming out of the sky. It said, "You are my Son. I love you, and I am proud of you." No one had ever heard of anything like this happening before. Everybody believed it was the voice of God.

Sometime later one of the crowd asked, "Where is that special man John baptized?"

"You mean Jesus?" another asked.

"Yeah, that's the one. He's from up in Galilee," the first man answered.

No one remembered for certain what time it was when he left. But someone had seen Jesus walking from the valley toward the rugged mountains close by. It may have been the wilderness mountain area near the ancient city of Jericho. No one seemed to understand why he wanted to go there. Someone suggested, "Maybe he was led there by God's Spirit."

"What do you mean by that," a young man asked.

The older man replied, "Haven't you ever felt there was something God wanted you to do? It's not something anyone asked you to do. It's an urge inside you to do something different than what you had expected to do" Others nodded in agreement and the young man was satisfied.

After he left, Jesus was not seen for 40 days. He was out there all by himself except for the animals and the angels who took care of him. Satan, also called the devil, tried to get him to do things that he was not supposed to do.

Oh, do you remember I mentioned that John the Baptist said things that made people mad? Well, there was this one person who had enough power to have him arrested, and he did.

After John was arrested and put in prison, Jesus walked back north to the country of Galilee. He went to his hometown, Nazareth, which was a village of about 1500 people. It was not long after he got home that Jesus told the people in Nazareth that it was time to begin God's Kingdom. He told them they should repent and quit sinning. He wanted them to believe the good news from God that he was sharing with them.

Before long Jesus moved from Nazareth to Capernaum a distance of about 20 miles. This was a village on the northwest shore of the Sea of Galilee. It was a great place for fishermen to live. Some of the best fishing in the area was between the cities of Bethsaida and Capernaum. Lots of fish were caught there, and some of them were sent to all parts of the Roman Empire.

The Romans also called the Sea of Galilee the Sea of Tiberius. It was a large beautiful lake about 13 miles long and a little more than 7 miles wide. In some places it was as much as 150 feet deep. Its water was very sweet and good to drink.

This lake was in a wonderful spot with mountains on both sides. The mountains between Nazareth and the Sea of Galilee were 2000 feet above the lakeshore. The slope of the mountains down to the lake was very steep. It was only about a half mile from the end of the mountain path down to the lakeshore.

One day Jesus was walking on the beach near Bethsaida. He saw Simon and his brother, Andrew, out in their boats fishing with nets. This was how they made a living. Jesus called to them and told them that they could become a new kind of fishermen.

He said, "If you will come with me, you will learn how to catch men and women instead of fish." Without even asking questions, they stopped what they were doing and went with him. They joined Jesus and together they walked a little farther down the beach. Jesus saw James and his brother, John, sons of a fisherman named Zebedee. They were in their boat, and they were fixing their fishing nets.

Jesus invited them to come with him, too. James and John immediately left their father and his hired men and also went with Jesus.

When the brothers left so quickly, I suppose those hired hands wondered what was going on. I surely would have. In those days even the boss's sons didn't leave the job before regular quitting time. I'm not sure how well the brothers knew Jesus, but they went with him anyway.

They just kept going and it wasn't long before the other fishermen realized the two brothers really were through fishing at Zebedee's. I'm not sure what Zebedee thought about this either. Jesus and the four men continued walking along the seashore until they finally reached the city of Capernaum.

In those days, the Jewish people worshiped on Saturday which they called the Sabbath. They worshiped God in a building that they called a synagogue. One Sabbath, Jesus walked into the synagogue in Capernaum and began to teach. The people were surprised because he taught the lesson better than their regular teachers in the synagogue did.

While Jesus was teaching, a man who was filled with an evil spirit screamed at him. "Why are you here?" he asked. "Do you want to destroy us? I know who you are. You are the Son of God."

To the evil spirit Jesus said, "Be quiet and come out of this man right now!"

The evil spirit shook the man and screamed once more, "Why are you here?" Then it left him.

Everyone was so surprised. They asked each other, "What happened? This new teacher has great power. He can even make evil spirits obey him!" Very quickly, all of the people in the land of Galilee heard about what Jesus had done.

Later Jesus went home with Simon and Andrew along with James and John. Simon's wife was waiting for them at the door to the house. "Oh, I'm so glad you got here in time," she said. "Mother has a high fever. I don't know what more to do."

"Where is she?" Jesus asked. Simon and his wife took Jesus

to her room and he healed her. Immediately she felt well and got up and fixed dinner for them.

The news of the miracle quickly spread. That evening, sick people and those who had evil spirits came to Jesus. They came so he could make them well, too. Soon all the people from the town were standing in front of Simon's house.

"Where is the healer?" they asked. "May we see him? Our loved ones need to be healed."

Jesus healed many of the people who came. He sent many evil spirits away and told those evil spirits not to talk about the fact that he was God's Son. He didn't want people to know that yet.

Early the next morning, Jesus got up and went back to the desert so he could be alone to pray. The people from the village didn't know that he was gone and they came to Simon's home looking for him.

"Simon, we need to see Jesus," they said.

"I'm sorry, but he left early this morning," he said.

"When will he be back?" they asked as they pushed forward toward the house. "We have more sick people here. We need him." There was nothing Simon or the other disciples could do but send them home.

When the neighbors left, the disciples talked among

17

themselves. "Did he say when he was coming back?" one asked.

"Not that I know of," another replied. "Do you know where he went? Did he tell anyone where he was going?"

"He didn't say, but I think we can find him," was the response. Then the disciples set out to find him.

When they found him out there in the desert, they told him, "Jesus, the people from the village showed up at Simon's house this morning looking for you. They wanted their friends and family members healed. Will you go back and help?"

"No," Jesus said, "I'll not be going back there now. I want to teach in other places, too. Let's go to other villages." In the days that followed, he and his disciples traveled to many places in the land of Galilee. He taught the people, healed many, and sent away evil spirits.

In one of the places they visited, a man who had a very dangerous skin disease called leprosy came to Jesus. He got on his knees and begged, "Jesus, I know you are able. If you want to, I know you are able to make me well."

Jesus cared very much about the man. He said, "I do want to." He touched the man and said, "Be well." The disease went away that very minute and his skin was smooth and healthy again. It was as if he had never been sick.

Jesus told the man to go straight to the priest, his minister, to show him that he was well. He was to take an offering to express his thanks to God for getting well. The man was not supposed to talk to anyone else.

He didn't do what Jesus asked him to do. Instead, the man went around telling everyone how Jesus had healed him. It wasn't long before a lot of people had heard what Jesus had done. To avoid the people, Jesus had to start living way out in some lonely places.

The people even found him there.

Chapter 2

It wasn't long before Jesus went back to Capernaum. The people quickly heard that he was there, and many came to where he was staying. There were so many they couldn't all get to the doorway of the house. As usual, Jesus willingly taught those who could hear him.

Once while he was teaching, four men carried a paralyzed man to him on a stretcher. "Can you believe this?" one of the four men asked.

"Who would have thought this many people would show up?" another of the four asked. "I thought we were the first ones to hear about Jesus coming to town."

"You know how news travels!" the third commented. "What are we going to do? There is no way we will be able to get him through the front door. Look at the crowd!"

"Well," the fourth man added, "there is no reason to ask people to let us through. Some of them look pretty sick."

"Hey, guys," the man on the stretcher spoke, "don't give up. Jesus is my only hope. You know that. We've tried every doctor and home remedy we know."

"Don't worry," the first man spoke again. "We are not giving up. We'll lay you on the ground while we check out the situation." They carefully placed the stretcher in a grassy spot. One stayed with the crippled man while the other three went to investigate. It was not long before the three returned.

"What's the solution?" the man who had stayed asked the other three.

"It will take a little work, but we can do it," one answered. "We found the stairway to the roof. You know how most of these houses are. It will be easy to take off a part of the roofing and let him right down in front of Jesus." They started working.

"Hey, look there," exclaimed one of the men in the room below. "Someone is taking off the roof." You could hear the buzz in the crowd as word traveled about what the men were doing.

"That's just part of it," someone else added. "I just saw them pass the window. I think they've got a man on a stretcher with them." The ohs and ahs were heard everywhere.

The men finished removing part of the roof. Slowly the

four men lowered the man on the stretcher down in front of Jesus. He saw how much the paralyzed man believed that he could be healed and he said to the man, "My son, your sins are forgiven." What a powerful statement!

The Pharisees, who were watching everything that was happening, were very upset with Jesus. They knew that only God could forgive sins. In their opinion, Jesus had no right to say that, but they didn't say anything.

Jesus knew what they were thinking. He asked them, "Is it easier to say, your sins are forgiven, or to say, pick up your bed, and walk?" This made the Pharisees even more angry. They couldn't think of any good way to answer his question.

Jesus was ready now for the people to know that he was the Son of God. He wanted them to understand that he could forgive sins and heal people. He had already forgiven the man's sins, so he said to the paralyzed man, "Get up. Pick up your stretcher and go home."

The man slowly got up, bent over and picked up his stretcher. They made room for him to get through the crowd. As he walked out in front of everyone, the people were really surprised and praised God for this miracle. They had never seen anything like this happen before.

Later, when Jesus went out by the lake a crowd came to him, and once more he taught them. While they were walking on the beach, he saw Levi sitting at his desk near the fishing boats. He was the man who collected taxes from the people. Jesus invited him to be one of his disciples. Levi, the son of Alphaeus, was excited and jumped up and went with Jesus right away. Since Levi worked for the Romans, they had given him the Roman name Matthew.

Jesus and his disciples went to Levi's house for dinner. Other tax collectors were there, too. Some of these people were well known for their bad behavior. Many of them who had been doing sinful things were now followers of Jesus. The Pharisees were upset when they saw Jesus eating with these people that they thought were bad. It was not long before they went to the disciples to complain. "Why is your Teacher having dinner with such bad people?" they asked.

When Jesus heard them talking, he called over to them, "You should know that sick people are the ones who need a doctor — not well people. I didn't come to help the good people repent. I came to help the sinners."

Then the Pharisees reminded him in a nasty manner, "Well, the religious leaders go without eating sometimes. Even John the Baptist and some of his followers did it." They did this as a special kind of religious activity called fasting. "Why don't you and your disciples do this, too?"

Jesus answered, "It's like this. When people go to a wedding and the groom is there, they don't refuse to eat the food offered to them. They are happy to be with the groom and his bride. They want to celebrate with them. Later the wedding will be over and the groom and his bride will be gone. That will be the time for them to fast."

The Pharisees were not pleased, but everyone else smiled at the answer.

Jesus continued, "If you are sewing up a hole in old clothes, you don't use some pretty new material to fix it. The old clothes would just tear away from the new patch. The rip would be worse than it was before. Surely you know that."

You could feel the tension rising among the religious leaders, but Jesus kept talking. "Farmers don't pour new wine into old wine containers made out of dried leather," he said. "If they did, the old containers would rip and tear. The wine would leak out, and there wouldn't be any good wine left. You all know that!"

The Pharisees had no response.

Sometime later on another Sabbath day, Jesus and his disciples were walking through a wheat field. They picked some of it to eat. The religious leaders said, "Look, your disciples are breaking the rules for the Sabbath day."

Jesus said, "Did you ever read what your great King David

did centuries ago when he and his friends were hungry? They went into God's house when Abiathar was the High Priest. David and his friends ate the bread that was supposed to be saved for only the priests to eat. That was surely breaking rules!"

"The Sabbath day was made to help us. We were not made to help the Sabbath day. I can decide what is allowed to be done on the Sabbath," Jesus said.

Chapter 3

❧

Once when Jesus went into the synagogue on the Sabbath a man was there who had a crippled hand. The Pharisees were there too, of course. As usual, they watched and listened very carefully to see what Jesus would do and say.

They believed it was wrong to do things on the Sabbath day. They even thought it was wrong to heal people on this holy day. The eyes of the Pharisees were on Jesus to see what he was going to do. Would he heal someone on this day? If he did, they were going to try to get him arrested for breaking one of their laws.

"You there with the crippled hand," Jesus called to the man who had the crippled hand. "Please come to the front of the synagogue." The man stood up and started forward.

When the man got close to him, Jesus looked over at the Pharisees. "I have two questions for you," he said to them. "Is it right to do good or is it right to do harm? Is it right to save a life or is it right to kill someone?" Nobody answered him.

Jesus continued to look at the Pharisees. He was very upset because they didn't care that a man had a problem with his

hand. He was angry with them because their religion would not let them care enough about other people to help them.

Jesus said to the man, "Stretch out your hand." The man did, and Jesus healed it. It was just as good as anybody else's hand. The Pharisees were so angry because Jesus healed a man on their holy day that they left at once. They went to talk with the

Jewish politicians who didn't like Jesus either. They all talked together about how they could get rid of him.

After this happened Jesus and his disciples left to go to the seashore. They wanted to get away by themselves. A large crowd of people followed them as usual. The fame of Jesus was spreading, and people were coming from many different places to see him.

Some walked from the far corners of Galilee. Others traveled miles from the Kingdom of Judea. Some came from the city of Jerusalem, and a place even farther south called Idumaea. Still others came from the northern cities of Tyre and Sidon up in the country of Phoenicia. All these people came to Jesus because they heard about what he was doing.

He told his disciples to have a small boat ready for him in case the crowd pushed in too close. Jesus had healed many people so lots of their friends who were sick kept trying to get near him. They shoved and pushed because they wanted to touch him. They thought if they could just touch him or if he would touch them they would be well.

When people who had evil spirits came near Jesus, the evil spirits would yell, "You are the Son of God!" Jesus told the evil spirits that they must not tell the people who he was.

Later Jesus went to the top of a hill. He had picked twelve special friends and invited them to go with him. They were to be his disciples and travel with him. They would become preachers and would have the power to send away evil spirits. These are the twelve men he chose:

Peter (also known as Simon)

James (a son of Zebedee)

John (another son of Zebedee)

Andrew (Peter's brother)

Philip

Bartholomew

Matthew (also known as Levi)

Thomas

James (a son of Alphaeus)

Thaddaeus

Simon (from the land of Canaan)

Judas Iscariot

On another day, Jesus went into a house and once more a crowd of people came to see him. Because there were so many, Jesus was really busy, and he forgot to eat.

When his brothers and other members of his family heard he was too busy to eat, they were really upset. They thought he was crazy, so they came to take care of him.

In the crowd were Pharisees who came from Jerusalem to watch Jesus. They said that Jesus had an evil spirit named Beelzebub inside of him. Because he could make evil spirits leave, they believed Jesus had the power of the prince of evil spirits. They were sure he was one of the most important of all the evil spirits.

Jesus spoke to the Pharisees and explained things to them by telling them stories. These stories were called parables. This time he began his story by asking the religious leaders, "How can the prince of evil spirits make other evil spirits go away?"

He didn't give them a chance to answer. He kept right on talking and told them some really important things. Here is a list of the things he told them:

1. If all the people in a country were fighting each other, the country would be ruined.

2. If a home were filled with fighting, it would be ruined.

3. If Satan were fighting against himself, he wouldn't be able to survive.

4. If a strong man was in a house, no one could take anything out of the house without tying up the strong man first.

Jesus explained these things because the religious leaders said he was doing miracles by Satan's power. He wanted to be certain that they knew that he was doing miracles by the power of God.

While this was going on, his mother and his brothers were standing outside. They sent a message to Jesus asking him to come out and see them. Someone in the crowd told Jesus that some of his family were outside.

Jesus asked the crowd, "Who is my mother? Who are my brothers?"

As he looked around the room, he said, "Here are my mother and my brothers." He explained that all people who do what God wants them to do are a mother or a brother or a sister to him.

Chapter 4

❧⨾❧

A few days later Jesus began teaching again at the beach by the lake. The crowd stood around the edge of the water as close to Jesus as they could get. There were so many people that Jesus

had to get in a boat and sit down. Then he told them many parables.

This is one of the parables he told. "A farmer went out to plant a garden. When he was putting the seeds in the ground, some of them dropped on the road. The birds came and ate them.

"Some of the seeds dropped on the rocks where the soil wasn't very good. Because the rocks were in the way, the seeds couldn't grow good roots. Since they didn't have deep roots, they couldn't get the water that they needed. When the sun made the plants real hot, they died.

"Some of the seeds dropped into the weeds. The weeds took up most of the food and water. There wasn't enough left for the seeds, so the plants from these seeds died.

"Some seeds went right into the good ground that was well prepared. When the plants grew, they were very healthy. In fact, they were so healthy that there were 30 or 60 or even 100 times more grains than usual from those seeds."

Then Jesus asked, "Were you listening to what I just told you?" He wanted to know if they were really paying attention. But no one answered him.

When he was alone with his twelve special friends, the disciples, they said, "We don't understand. What did the parable about the seeds mean?"

He replied, "Other people just hear the parables, but you get to know exactly what they mean. The parables are about God's Kingdom.

"In the Old Bible, God said that people would see and hear about His Kingdom, but they wouldn't understand it. Since they didn't understand it, they would not ask God to forgive them of their sins."

His disciples didn't say anything, so Jesus asked them if

36

they now knew the meaning of the parable about the seeds and the farmer. Everyone was really quiet. Each of his disciples seemed afraid to say anything.

Finally, he said to them, "If you didn't understand this parable about the farmer and the seeds, how will you understand other parables?" Without waiting for an answer he explained what the parable meant.

"The seeds are like God's Word," he began. "The farmer planting his garden is like a person who tells others what the Bible, God's Word, says.

"First," Jesus continued, "think about the seeds that fell on the ground and were eaten by birds." He waited a moment before continuing, "Those seeds are like people who hear what God says. But Satan immediately comes along and makes them forget what they just heard. This happens when they hear about God and the Bible but don't pay attention to it. Because they were not really paying attention, they didn't find out how to be forgiven. God's Word wasn't important to them." Jesus paused.

The disciples looked at each other without saying anything. Each one knew it was really time for them to pay careful attention to what Jesus was teaching.

Jesus started again. "The seeds that fell on the rocks and couldn't grow good roots are like people who seem very glad to hear about God's Word. They pay attention so they can feel good. But when the good feelings go away, they act just like they did before they heard the good news. When trouble and hard times come, they quit doing what's right. They forget everything they heard about God.

"The seeds that fell in the weeds are like people who were excited when they first heard about God's Word. But, in the story, the weeds used up all the good food and water so the seeds didn't have enough, and they died. That represents the people who start spending their time on other things.

"They don't take time to learn more about God. They worry about all kinds of things going on in their lives. They use a lot of their time and energy trying to get rich because they think that's what is really important. They dream about being rich, and they just keep wishing for more things. They try so hard to get all these things, and they don't have enough time or energy left to listen to God. So God's Word wasn't important to them any more."

Finally, Jesus told them about the seeds in the good soil that grew into such healthy plants. He said, "These seeds are like people who hear God's Word and want to learn more about God immediately. When they understood God's Word, they began doing the things it says to do. Their lives became more wonderful than they could imagine."

Jesus asked the disciples, "Does a lamp do any good if it is hiding under a bed? Isn't it put on a stand where it can be seen?" He continued, "When the light is shining, things won't be hidden because they can be seen with the light. There won't be any more secrets some day. God will explain all of them."

He told the disciples, "Don't just listen to what I am saying! I want you to fully understand what I'm talking about. If you really pay attention, you will learn more. When you don't pay close attention, its easy to forget the little bit you did know."

The disciples nodded that they understood the point he was making.

Jesus said, "The Kingdom of God is like a farmer who throws seed on the ground and then goes to bed for the night. When he wakes up each morning, he sees the seed is growing into a plant. He knows it has grown, but he doesn't know what made it grow.

"The seed comes up from the ground first as a little blade like grass. Then the plant gets bigger. Finally, the plant is full-grown and has a grain that is used for food. When the grain is ready, the farmer will come and pick the grain."

Jesus also told them another parable to explain what God's Kingdom was like. He said, "The Kingdom of God is like a mustard seed. Even though this seed is very, very small, when the seed grows up, it is the biggest plant in the garden with very large branches. If birds built a nest in this plant, they would have shade."

When people were around to hear Jesus teach, he would tell them parables about God. Afterwards, when he was alone with the disciples, he would always explain the parables to them.

One evening Jesus asked his disciples to go to the other side of the lake. They left the crowd and got into a boat to go across the lake. About the time they reached the middle of the lake a storm came. Sudden storms were not unusual on the Sea of Galilee. The winds were very strong and the waves were so big and choppy that a lot of water got into the boat. Jesus was sleeping on a cushion in the bottom of the boat. The disciples woke him up and said, "Teacher, don't you care if we die?"

When he was wide awake, he looked up and spoke to the wind, "Be still." After he spoke, the wind quit blowing, and the sea was calm. Jesus asked, "Why were you afraid? Don't you trust me?"

The disciples were truly surprised about what Jesus had done. They said to each other, "Who is this person? He makes even the wind and the sea do what he says. Who is he?"

Chapter 5

࿐

On another day Jesus and the disciples sailed once more to the other side of the lake. This time they beached their boats in the land of the Gerasenes. This is one of the ten city-states in the country of Decapolis. Decapolis is a Greek word that means ten cities.

When Jesus got out of the boat, a man who lived in tombs came running to meet him. This man had evil spirits which made him do some very harmful and dangerous things. He was so dangerous that the people used to tie him up with chains. They did it so he couldn't hurt himself or anyone else. But the evil spirits inside him became so strong that he could break out of any chains they used. He spent all his time in the tombs and out on the hillsides yelling. He kept cutting himself with sharp rocks.

When he got to where Jesus was standing, he bowed in

front of him. The evil spirits inside of the man yelled at Jesus, "What do you want to do to me, Jesus, Son of the Most High God? Please, for God's sake, don't hurt me."

Jesus said to him, "What is your name?"

The evil spirits in the man answered, "Our name is Legion because there are so many of us." For some unknown reason the man begged Jesus not to send the evil spirits to another country.

About 2,000 pigs were eating on the hillside close by. The evil spirits said to Jesus, "If you are going to send us away, could we go into those pigs over there?"

"Go," he said. So the evil spirits came out of the man and went into the pigs. The pigs then ran down the hill and went right out into the sea. They drowned.

The people that took care of the pigs ran away. They rushed back into town and told the same message to everyone they saw. "You won't believe what just happened. The crazy man is sane, and our pigs are drowned." Lots of people decided to go see for themselves.

When the people came to Jesus, they were surprised at what they saw. There was the man who had the evil spirits sitting quietly nearby. He was dressed, and his mind was back to normal. The people were afraid. Those who had seen what happened told those who had just arrived about how the evil spirits left the man and went into the pigs.

The people were so frightened by all of this that they begged Jesus to go away from them. Jesus started back to the shore. As he was getting into the boat, the man who had been healed came to him. "Please, Jesus, may I go with you?"

Jesus replied, "No, you cannot go with me. Instead," he said, "please go home and tell everyone about the wonderful thing God did for you. Tell them how much God loves you."

The man did what Jesus asked him to do. He left the seashore area and went to the cities in the land of the Decapolis. He told the people what God had done for him. The people were truly amazed.

Once more Jesus and the disciples went back to where

they had come from on the other side of the lake. A very, very large group of people came to see him when he got there. This time he decided to stay by the shore of the lake.

One of the officers in the synagogue, Jairus, came to Jesus and bowed down at his feet. He said to him, "My little daughter is dying. Please come and put your hands on her so she can get well and live."

Immediately Jesus went with Jairus, and a large crowd followed them. In the crowd there was a woman who had a blood disease. She had been sick for twelve years. She had gone to many doctors and spent all the money she had. But, instead of getting better, she just kept getting worse. When she heard about Jesus, she joined others in looking for him. Now she had found him.

Even though the crowd was large, she pushed and shoved her way through. Finally, she was close to him. She thought to herself, "If I can just touch his clothes, I know I'll be made well." She waited for her chance.

When she thought no one was looking, she stretched out her hand. As soon as she touched his clothes, she knew the disease had left her body. She was well! Jesus knew immediately that his power to heal had helped someone at that very moment. He turned around to the crowd and asked, "Who touched my clothes?"

46

The disciples looked at each other and wondered why Jesus would ask a question like that?" He never asked anything like that before.

"The crowd is so big that people are constantly bumping into each other. We couldn't possibly know who touched you, Jesus," another added.

Nevertheless, Jesus looked around to see who had touched him. The woman who had been healed was afraid. Timidly she came and bowed down to Jesus. "I am the one, Jesus," she said. Then she told him how much she had suffered and how long she had been sick.

Jesus said, "Daughter, because you had faith to believe, you are well. Go in peace. You will stay well."

While Jesus was talking with her, people came from the house of Jairus. "You don't need to bother Jesus any more, Jarius. Your daughter is dead," they told him.

Jesus heard them. "Don't be afraid, Jairus. Just keep on believing."

When they were close to Jairus' house, Jesus took Peter, James and his brother, John, and went ahead of the crowd. When they arrived at the house where Jairus lived, people there were crying very loudly. Jesus asked, "Why are you crying? The child has not died, but she is asleep."

They were shocked at his words. They stopped crying and began laughing at him.

Jesus then made everyone leave except Peter, James, John, and the girl's father and mother. He went into the room where the child was lying. He took her hand and said words that meant, "Little girl, I ask you to get up."

At that very minute, the girl opened her eyes, got up, and began to walk around the house. She was twelve years old. Everyone was amazed!

Jesus spoke to them, "Please do not tell others about this. She is well. I do think you should give her something to eat."

Chapter 6

ॐॐ

Jesus and his disciples went back to his hometown, Nazareth. On the next Sabbath, he went to the synagogue there and began to teach. The people from his hometown were really surprised to hear what he was saying.

"How did he learn all these things?" they asked one another. "How can he possibly perform miracles? He's from around here. He's no different than we are." They were puzzled and had no answers. They began to share what they did know about him hoping that they might find some explanation.

"Why, he's just the village carpenter," one said.

"I know his mother, Mary," another added.

"His brothers are James, Joses, Judas and Simon," someone called out.

"Don't forget his sisters live down the street," another said.

Even though they all knew Jesus performed miracles it didn't matter. They were not able or willing to change their feelings or attitude about him. As far as they were concerned he was just the village carpenter. Yet, in the days that followed, the people of Nazareth continued to ask questions.

"What is so special about him? Why is everyone paying so much attention to him?" they asked. The people of Nazareth were unhappy because they couldn't understand why Jesus should be special. "He's just one of the men from the neighborhood who has lived around here for years."

Knowing all this Jesus said, "A man can be respected everywhere except in his home town or around his family."

He did heal a few people there, but Jesus was not able to do very many miracles in his hometown. Most of the people did not believe that he really was God's Son. He thought about their unbelief and it made him sad. He left his hometown and went to a nearby village where he was able to teach people about God.

When Jesus got his twelve disciples together again, he taught them how to get rid of evil spirits just like he did. He instructed them to travel with one other disciple whenever they were going some place to teach people about God. They were not to pack anything for their trips. All they needed to take was a cane to use for a walking stick to help them over the rough countryside.

"You are not to take any food or money. Take only the shoes you wear, and don't take extra clothes," he told them.

The disciples nodded.

Jesus continued, "When you get into a town, go to the house of one of my followers, and stay with them until it is time to leave that town. If you come to any place where people don't want to hear you or listen to you, don't worry about it. Instead, leave that place and go somewhere else."

So the disciples went out and taught people about God. They told them that they should ask God to forgive them for the things they did wrong. They also sent away evil spirits, and they helped many sick people get well.

King Herod heard about what the disciples of Jesus were doing. Some people told him, "John the Baptist has come back from the dead. He and his disciples are doing these miracles."

Other people said, "It's not John. This man is Elijah, an ancient prophet."

Some others claimed, "Oh, don't worry. It's neither Elijah nor John. This is just another prophet like we've had through the centuries."

But King Herod said, "It must be that John has come back to life! I had his head cut off." Herod remembered and was afraid.

Earlier King Herod had John the Baptist arrested and

put in prison because something he said made him mad. John had told him, "It is wrong for you to marry your brother's wife, Herodias." She was the wife of Herod's brother, Philip. Herodias was mad, too, because John said that to Herod. She wanted to kill John, but she couldn't because she lacked authority.

King Herod was actually afraid of John because he knew that he was a holy man. When he had heard John teach, he didn't understand him, but he liked to listen to him.

Finally, Herodias had a chance to get even. It was at Herod's birthday party. He invited a lot of important people to celebrate with him. During the party, Herodias' daughter danced for King Herod and his guests. The king was so pleased that he told the girl she could ask for anything, and he would give it to her. He said, "I'll give you anything you ask for up to half of my kingdom."

She asked her mother, "What shall I tell the king I want?"

Her mother knew this was her chance to get what she wanted. She answered, "Ask for the head of John the Baptist."

With that instruction, her daughter hurried back to the king and said, "I want you to give me John the Baptist's head right now."

The king was very sad and very sorry. It wasn't easy for a king to change his mind when he made a promise in front of his guests. So he sent word to the prison guards. He ordered them to

cut off John's head.

It was brought to Herodias' daughter on a platter. She took it, and then she gave this strange gift to her mother.

The news spread quickly about what had happened to John the Baptist. Hearing it, John's disciples came for his body. They buried it in a tomb.

When the disciples of Jesus returned from their travels, they gave a complete report. Jesus knew the disciples were very tired. There were so many people around them that they didn't even have a chance to eat. So he said to them, "Come away by yourselves to a quiet place and rest."

The disciples and Jesus took a boat and went away hoping to get away from the crowds. It didn't work out like the disciples thought it would. When the people saw where they were going, they hurried around the lake so they could be at the place where the boat would land.

When Jesus saw the big crowd, he felt sorry for them. He could see that they were like sheep that didn't have anyone to take care of them. He began to teach them many things.

He had been teaching quite a while, and it was getting late. Finally, his disciples came and talked with him. "Jesus, it will soon be time to eat. You should send the people away so that they can go to the villages and buy food. They need to eat."

Jesus answered, "You give them something to eat."

The disciples replied, "Do you want us to go and spend a lot of money on food so we can give them something to eat?"

Jesus answered, "How much food do you have? Go look and see." They came back and told Jesus what they had found. There were five loaves of bread and two fish.

Without explaining to the disciples what he was going to do, Jesus turned to the crowd. He told them to sit down on the grass in groups. Some of the people were in groups of 100 and others were in groups of 50.

After everyone had a place to sit, Jesus took the five loaves of bread and the two fish. He looked up to heaven and prayed for the food. Then he broke the loaves of bread and kept giving bread to the disciples. They were to give it to the people who were sitting down. Then he took the fish and kept giving fish to the disciples until all of the people had fish, too!

Every person there ate until they were full. After they had finished eating, the disciples collected the leftovers. It took twelve baskets to hold all the bread and fish that were left! Altogether

that food had fed over 5,000 men! No one bothered to count the women and children who were there that day.

Then Jesus had his disciples get into the boat and set sail for the town of Bethsaida. He stayed behind to tell all the people that it was time for them to go home. After he said goodbye, he went up the mountain to pray.

By evening, the boat that the disciples were using was in the middle of the lake. Jesus was by himself up on the mountain. He looked out across the lake, and he could tell that the disciples were having trouble. The wind was blowing against them, and they were having problems rowing against the wind and the waves.

At about four o'clock in the morning, Jesus decided to help them. He walked down from the mountain and just walked out on the water to where they were.

Remember that the disciples were grown men and not easily frightened. They knew how rough the lake could get in a storm, but that did not prepare them for what they saw.

They could not believe what was going on. Someone was walking on the water towards them. They thought he was going to walk right on by. When he came closer, they thought they saw a ghost. They were frightened and they cried out.

But Jesus spoke to them right away. "Have courage. It's me.

Don't be afraid," he called to them. Then he got into the boat with them, and the wind stopped blowing. The disciples were shocked.

It had been quite a day. The disciples didn't know how Jesus fed all of those people. Even though they were trying to understand, they were still confused. And now this! In the morning when the boat landed, they were at a place called Gennesaret. As soon as they were out of the boat, the people in the village recognized Jesus.

People from all around the country began to bring sick people to him. No matter where Jesus went, whether it was a village or a city or in the country, people came to him. They just wanted to touch his clothes so they could be well. And in fact, everyone who did touch him was healed.

Chapter 7

૭ન્ડ

One day some Pharisees and the Scribes, the religious leaders, came all the way from Jerusalem to see Jesus. They saw that some of his disciples were eating bread without following the religious rules for washing their hands first. The religious leaders had many rules!

These rules were passed from one generation to the next. There were special rules for washing your hands before eating. Ever since this special rule was started, religious people would never eat in the marketplace without following that rule. They even had a special way for washing cups, pitchers, copper pots, and other things.

The Pharisees asked, "Jesus, why don't your disciples follow the rules about washing their hands?"

Jesus replied, "Don't you remember what Isaiah wrote?"

He didn't give them a chance to answer.

He continued, "Isaiah wrote about people who talked about God but did not live the way they talked. Isaiah said that kind of a person is a hypocrite, a phony. He wrote that they worshiped God, but it didn't really mean anything to them. The religious leaders made their own laws and rules. They taught that they were God's laws and rules."

The Scribes and Pharisees were not hearing what they wanted to hear. But they had started this discussion, so they really couldn't leave while Jesus was still answering them.

Jesus continued, "You pushed aside God's commandments, His rules to live by, in order to follow your traditions. You want to do things like your ancestors always did them."

Without a moment's hesitation Jesus went on, "You know what Moses said. 'Honor your father and your mother' and 'People who spoke evil about their parents should die'.

"Of course that's what we teach," one of the Pharisees said to him.

Jesus ignored the comment and continued, "But you say it is

all right to tell your parents, 'I can't help you. What I would have given to you to help is gone. I've already given it to God.' Then you no longer do anything for your father or mother."

The Pharisees were embarrassed.

"That is man's rule," Jesus said. "It is opposite to God's rule which demands that children should take care of their parents." Jesus finished his comments by saying, "You religious leaders have a lot of rules like that."

Jesus called to the crowd of people who were standing around. "Listen to me — all of you — and understand what I say. What goes into a man from the outside is not what is important. These aren't the things that make him bad. The important thing is what comes out of the person. What comes out lets us know whether he is good or bad." Then Jesus left the crowd and went into the house where he was staying.

The disciples asked him, "What did you mean when you spoke to the people?"

Jesus replied, "Don't you men understand any better than the crowd? Can't you see that it doesn't matter what goes inside a man? It does not go into his heart. When a man eats something, it goes into his stomach, and his body takes care of it." Jesus was saying that all foods were good for eating.

"We know that," a disciple said.

Jesus explained to them, "I'm not talking about your physical heart that pumps blood. I'm talking about your spiritual heart. That's how you decide whether to do right or to do wrong. A person isn't bad because he eats something that the religious rules don't approve. He is bad when he decides to do wrong."

Then Jesus mentioned some of the bad things that people sometimes do:

- think bad thoughts
- have sex with a person who is not their husband or wife
- steal what belongs to someone else
- kill someone
- treat their husband or wife wrongly
- get upset because other people have things they want
- lie
- put too much importance on how their body might look to other people
- go around saying bad things about people
- think they are better than everyone else
- make decisions that are not wise.

Jesus explained that all of these things were wrong. People were bad because they decided to do or say or think bad things.

Soon Jesus left and went to Tyre, an ancient Phoenician city. Tyre is a very important seaport on the coast of the

Mediterranean Sea. When he arrived there, he tried to go unnoticed to the house where he was going to stay. But it didn't work.

A woman had a little daughter with an evil spirit. When she heard that Jesus was in town, she came to him and bowed down at his feet. "Jesus, my daughter has an evil spirit inside of her. We can't control it, but I know you can. Will you please send the evil spirit away?"

Jesus did not reply immediately. The woman was a Phoenician, a Gentile, not a Jew. Yet, she was asking a special favor from this Jewish teacher. She was not discouraged because Jesus didn't respond at once. She wanted help. She was willing to beg for that help if she had too.

But Jesus said to her, "Children should get to eat first and have all they want before the leftovers are given to the dogs."

What he meant by this strange answer was clear to her.

Jesus would give help to his people first. So she answered him, "Even dogs get to eat the scraps that fall on the floor."

Jesus listened to her response. "You have answered well. When you get home, you will see that your daughter doesn't have an evil spirit any more." She went back home and found her daughter just as he had promised.

Jesus then left Tyre for the city of Sidon. This is about twenty miles further north on the Mediterranean coast. After spending some time there he went back south and east to the region of the Decapolis along the eastside of the Sea of Galilee.

One day after he arrived, people brought a man to Jesus. "This man cannot hear at all," they said. "He also has trouble speaking. Will you please touch him so he can be well?"

Jesus took the man away from the crowd. First, he put his fingers in the man's ears. Next, he spit and got saliva on his finger and touched the man's tongue with it. Then Jesus looked up to heaven and with a deep sigh he said to him, "Ephphatha." In the local language that meant, "Be opened." At that very minute the man could hear. He didn't have any more trouble talking either.

When he and the man went back to the crowd, Jesus said, "The man is well. Please don't tell anyone that I have made him well."

They didn't obey him. The more Jesus wanted it to be a secret, it seemed the more the crowd wanted to tell everyone. The people were very, very excited. They wanted to talk about the good things Jesus did. "When people are deaf, he can make them able to hear. When people can't talk very well, he can help them to talk just as well as anyone," they said.

Chapter 8

ॐ

There was another time when a great crowd of people had come to listen to Jesus. They had nothing to eat. Jesus said to his disciples, "I care very much about these people because they have listened to me for three days, and they have nothing to eat. If I send them home without eating, some of them will faint. Some live a long way from here!"

The disciples asked, "Where can we find enough bread to feed all these people in this wilderness?"

"How many loaves of bread do you have?" Jesus asked.

"We have seven loaves," they answered.

Jesus told the people to sit down on the ground. Then he took the seven loaves and thanked God for them. He broke pieces from the loaves and gave them to the disciples who took them to the people. Everyone in the large crowd got enough bread to eat.

The disciples also had found a few small fish. After Jesus thanked God for the fish, he told the disciples to serve them to the crowd. All of the people — there were about 4,000 — ate until they were satisfied. The disciples collected seven baskets of food that were left over. After everyone had finished eating, Jesus sent them home.

He and his disciples immediately got into a boat and went to a part of the country called Dalmanutha. As usual the religious leaders showed up and started to argue with Jesus. They wanted proof that he really could make miracles happen.

Jesus gave a big sigh and said, "Why are these people who are living right now asking for some kind of proof? How many more miracles do they need? No more proof is going to be given to them."

Jesus left there with the disciples and started back to the other side of the lake. He began talking to the them about yeast. "Beware of the yeast of Herod and the Pharisees," Jesus warned.

When the disciples heard him talk about yeast, they became worried because they didn't have enough bread on the boat for their next meal. Yeast is used in making bread soft by changing the way the ingredients act together. They began talking among themselves about how they had forgotten to bring more bread. They only had one loaf with them in the boat.

Jesus listened to what they were saying. Finally, he asked, "Why are you worried about the bread? Don't you understand? Don't you believe what I have to say? Are you blind? Don't you hear anything? Don't you remember when I used five loaves of bread to feed 5,000 people? How many baskets of food did you pick up after everyone was fed?"

"Twelve," they answered.

Jesus continued, "Just now, when I used the seven loaves of bread to feed 4,000, how many baskets of food was left for you to pick up?"

"Seven," they muttered.

"Don't you understand yet?" he asked. No one answered. Finally, they reached the village of Bethsaida.

As usual the people came looking for Jesus, and once more they brought people who needed to be healed. They called to Jesus, "This man is blind. Won't you please have mercy on him and make him see again?" they begged.

Jesus took the man's hand and led him out of the village.

He put spit on the man's eyes, touched them, and then asked the man, "Do you see anything?"

The man answered, "I see men, but they look like trees walking around." Jesus put his hands on the man's eyes again. This time the man could see perfectly. Jesus told him not to go back to the village but to go straight home instead.

The disciples and Jesus left there and went to visit other villages near the city of Caesarea Philippi which is about thirty miles from Bethsaida. On the way, Jesus asked them, "Who do people say that I am?"

"Well, there is certainly a difference of opinion on that!" one responded. Several began speaking at the same time.

"Some people think you are John the Baptist."

"Others say you are Elijah."

"But some others think you are another one of the prophets."

Jesus continued by asking, "But who do *you* say that I am?"

Immediately Peter answered, "You are the Christ, the Son of God. Hundreds of years ago our forefathers were promised you would come."

"You must be very careful. Do not tell that to anyone yet," Jesus said. He continued in a very serious tone of voice. "In the future, the religious leaders will be against me. They will even have me killed."

He saw the sad looks on each man's face and said, "Please don't get discouraged. I will be alive again in three days." He was trying very hard to help his disciples understand what would be happening in the near future.

Peter took him to the side and argued, "Jesus, surely you must be wrong! Nothing like that can possibly happen to you."

Jesus turned back around and looked at the disciples. Then he told Satan to leave because Peter was talking about man's way instead of God's way.

Soon after that Jesus asked a great crowd of people to join him and the disciples. He said to all of them, "If you want to follow me, you must give up what you want. You must choose what I want for you. It doesn't matter what that is. You can decide what you're going to do with your life, and if you decide not to follow me, in the end you will have nothing. You should let me control your life. Live as I ask you to live. Tell others about me. If you do, in the end you'll have everything."

Jesus continued. "You can spend your whole life doing what

pleases you. You might even possibly get everything you want. What's it worth, if you can't be with me when you die?"

"Some people are ashamed of me in this world. They'll be sorry later because then I will be ashamed of them. That will take place when they come to be with God the Father and His holy angels."

Jesus told the crowd, "It is true. Some of you will see the power of God's Kingdom before you die." This was another time Jesus said something they did not understand.

Chapter 9

Six days later, Jesus took Peter, James, and John with him to the top of a mountain. The disciples had no idea why they were going there, and they were in for a real surprise.

While they were on the mountaintop, they saw a change in the way Jesus looked. "Look at that!" one of the disciples exclaimed. "Look at Jesus! Have you ever seen clothes that glow like that?"

"I certainly have never seen clothes that white!" was the reply. None of them could explain what was happening right there in front of them. The three had not even understood what they had just seen before something even stranger happened.

Two more men suddenly appeared on the mountain top. The disciples had no idea where these men had come from or how they got there. Jesus was talking with the men, and they didn't want to interrupt him. So, there they stood, with no one to explain what was happening.

"Can you believe this?" a disciple whispered. Pointing to one of the men who had suddenly appeared, he continued, "That must be Elijah and the other one..."

A second disciple interrupted him with, "That's Moses!"

The third disciple added, "Those are two of the most important leaders in our Jewish history!"

Still in a state of shock the first disciple said, "They lived hundreds of years ago. What is happening to us?"

I cannot explain how the three disciples were able to recognize that it was Elijah and Moses. But it was true that these men had lived hundreds of years earlier. The Old Bible includes books written by Moses, and other writers in the Old Bible had written about Elijah.

Peter, James, and John were truly thrilled to have the privilege of being at this special meeting. Peter, as usual, was the spokesman for the disciples. He couldn't keep quiet any longer. "This is really exciting, Jesus. Why, it would be wonderful if we could build three chapels for worship here on the mountain. We could build one for you, and one for Moses, and one for Elijah."

Jesus didn't answer. In the silence the disciples became very afraid — especially when a cloud came over all of them. A voice from the cloud announced, "This is my son. I love him very much. Listen to him."

Stunned, the disciples looked around. They were surprised to discover there was no one with them except Jesus. Moses and Elijah were gone. How they left was just as much a mystery as how they got there in the first place.

As they were coming down the mountain, Jesus talked with them. "Men, you must not tell anyone what you have just seen. It must not be shared until after I have been raised from the dead."

They continued down the mountain. Finally, one of the disciples broke the silence. "I'm confused," he said.

"Me, too," added the second, and the third disciple nodded in agreement. Not one of them understood what Jesus meant when he said he would be raised from the dead.

They talked among themselves about this strange idea, and then they asked, "What do the religious leaders mean when they say that Elijah must come first?"

Jesus explained, "Elijah had said that a prophet would come before the Messiah appeared. John the Baptist was that prophet. The people treated him badly just like the Old Bible said they would!" At that moment the disciples knew exactly what had happened to John the Baptist and why.

Jesus continued, "What you really need to understand is that I will be suffering much. I will be treated cruelly in the coming days."

When Jesus, Peter, James, and John got back to the rest of the disciples, a crowd was there. Some religious leaders in the crowd were arguing with the disciples. When the crowd saw Jesus, they were excited and ran to him, and he asked, "What have you been talking about that makes you so excited?"

A man responded, "Teacher, I brought my son who has an evil spirit that keeps him from being able to talk. When it bothers him, it makes him fall down. Foam starts coming out of his mouth. He grinds his teeth, and his body gets very stiff. I asked your disciples to make the evil spirit leave my son, but they couldn't."

Jesus declared, "Oh, you people who won't believe what is true! How long will I be with you? How long should I have to keep helping you? Bring him to me."

They brought the boy to him. As soon as he saw Jesus, the evil spirit made the boy's body shake really hard, and he fell on the ground, rolled around, and foam started coming out of his mouth.

Jesus asked the boy's father, "How long has this been happening?"

"Since he was a child," he answered. "The evil spirit has

often tried to kill him by making him fall in fire or in water. If you can do anything, please help us."

Jesus said to him, "If I can? All things are possible to the person who believes!"

Quickly the man declared, "I believe. Please help me to believe more." Jesus saw that people were in a hurry to get close. He said to the evil spirit, "You, spirit that can't hear and can't speak, I order you to come out of this boy. You cannot go into him again!"

After yelling and making the boy shake very hard, the evil spirit came out. It looked like the boy was dead. People even said he was dead, but Jesus took the boy's hand and helped him get up.

When the disciples were in the house alone with Jesus, they asked him, "Why couldn't we make the evil spirit leave that boy?"

"You can't do it in your own power. There isn't any way to get that kind of evil spirit out except to pray," Jesus answered.

Before long they left there and began to travel through Galilee. Once more Jesus didn't want anyone to know about where they were going. He wanted to use this time to teach the disciples. "Men, you must understand what I am telling you. I am going to be arrested and killed. Three days after I am killed, I will come back to life."

They could not understand what he meant at all. But his words were so frightening that they were afraid to ask him.

When they reached Capernaum, he inquired, "What were you talking about on the way here?" They were quiet for a long time. They didn't want to answer him. They were embarrassed because they had been talking about which one of them was the greatest.

Jesus sat down and had the twelve disciples sit around him. "So you want to be first?" he asked. "That's a real challenge. If you want to be the greatest you must help everyone else. By the time you get all that done you will be in last place."

They entered the house where they were staying and a child

was there. Jesus had him come and stand with them. He hugged the child, and as he did he spoke to his disciples, "When you accept a child in my name, you are accepting me. When you accept me, you are really accepting God who sent me."

John said, "Teacher, we saw someone who was using your name to make evil spirits leave people. Since he wasn't part of our group, we made him stop."

Jesus responded, "Don't make people stop doing that. If they are doing things with the power from my name, they are not going to say bad things about me. People who are not against us are on our side. People will want to help you because you are my disciples. Some may only give you a drink of water, but they will still get a reward."

The disciples were a little surprised by what Jesus was saying. They had never realized that other people could do the good things Jesus was teaching them to do. For a moment they quit listening and talked among themselves. Jesus got their attention again when he said, "If someone makes it hard for a child to keep believing in me, it would be better if that person had drowned." Then they understood how important children were to Jesus.

"If a hand makes you do bad things, it would be better not to have the hand," Jesus said. "If a foot makes you go to bad places, it would be better not to have the foot. If an eye watches bad things, it would be better not to have the eye. When you make choices that lead you to hell, it is much worse than being crippled. Hell is the most awful place! The fire never dies down!"

Everyone will go through difficult situations to help get rid of those things in life that are not pleasing to God. It is way salt is used to make the sacrifice pure.

Jesus compared people to salt. He said that if salt quits being salty, it wouldn't do any good. If we are effective salt we will be able to live at peace with others.

These were some more of the things that Jesus taught his disciples.

Chapter 10

❧❧

Some time later Jesus got up and walked down along the Jordan River to Judea. When he got there, crowds surrounded him again. As usual, he began to teach them. The Pharisees soon let him know they were there. As usual they tried to make trouble. They asked, "Is it against the law for a man to divorce his wife."

Jesus responded, "What did Moses tell you to do?"

They replied, "Moses said a man was allowed to divorce his wife and send her away."

Jesus told them, "God allowed divorce because people's hearts were not pure. But from the very beginning, when God made man and woman, His plan was for them to leave their parents and marry. They would no longer have two separate lives. Instead, they would be one family. When God joined them together at their wedding, He intended for them to be married to each other as long as they lived. He didn't want anyone to do anything that would cause them to be separated ever again."

After they had gone into the house where they were staying, the disciples asked Jesus again about this. He answered, "If a man divorces his wife and marries another woman, he commits adultery. Adultery happens when a man has sex with a woman who is married to another man."

That discussion ended when people began coming to the house and bringing their children so Jesus could touch them. The disciples strongly disapproved of Jesus being bothered by children. They had already forgotten how important Jesus said children were. When Jesus saw his disciples were trying to keep children away from him, he was upset. He told them, "Let the children come to me. Don't stop them. Children show what it takes to belong to the Kingdom of God. It is important that you understand that you cannot be a part of the Kingdom of God unless you are like a child."

Then he took the children in his arms and blessed them as he laid his hands on them.

A few days later Jesus was leaving on a trip. He stopped when a man ran up to him and knelt in front of him. The man began, "Good Teacher, what shall I do so that I can live forever?"

Jesus answered, "Why do you call me good? God is the only

one who is good. But to answer your question, you know the commandments — do not murder, do not commit adultery, do not steal, do not lie, respect your parents."

The man then stated, "Teacher, I have kept all these commandments since I was young."

Jesus looked at the man. He felt love for him and said quietly, "Then there is just one thing you need to do. Go and sell everything you have and give the money to poor people. But don't worry; you will have things of great value in heaven. Then come and follow me."

When the man heard these words, he felt very bad. He walked away from Jesus, and he was really sad. He owned a lot of property, and he didn't want to sell it.

Jesus turned to his disciples, "It is very hard for rich people to become part of God's Kingdom."

The disciples were surprised. "You must understand," he told them, "if you are rich and love being rich, it's very hard to be

83

part of God's Kingdom. In fact, it's easier for a camel to go through the eye of a needle than for a rich person to become part of God's Kingdom."

The disciples were even more surprised and asked, "Then who can be saved?"

Jesus looked at them and said, "It is impossible for men. But God does impossible things. Nothing is too hard for Him."

Peter said to Jesus, "We left everything we had to come and follow you."

Jesus encouraged him with this reply. "If you have given up homes, or family, or friends, or other things for me or for the gospel, you will not lose out. Instead, you will gain hundreds of friends, family, homes, and other things. But, you will also have troubles. The best part is that you will live forever in heaven. Many people who try to be first will be last, and those willing to be last will be first."

As Jesus led them on the road from Galilee to Jerusalem, the disciples were amazed at his teaching. Even though Jesus was walking along with them, the people were afraid.

He took the twelve aside and began to tell them what was going to happen to him. He said, "We are going to Jerusalem. The chief priests and Scribes there are going to take me, and they will order me to be killed. They will give me to the Romans who will make fun of me and they'll even spit on me. They will beat me with a whip and then kill me. Three days later I will come back to life."

The disciples were extremely quiet and thought seriously about what he had just said.

James and John, who were Zebedee's sons, came up to Jesus and said, "Teacher, there is something we want you to do for us."

"What is it that you want me to do for you?" he asked.

They answered, "When you are in your glory, may we sit on your right side and on your left side?"

Jesus replied, "You don't understand what you are asking. Do you think you are able to drink the cup I drink? Are you able to be baptized the way that I am going to be baptized?" He was asking them if they were willing to suffer like he was going to suffer.

They said, "We are."

Jesus said to them, "Then you will drink the cup I drink, and you will be baptized the way I am baptized. But I am not the one who will decide who sits on my right hand and my left hand. Those places are being prepared for the people God has chosen."

When the rest of the disciples found out what James and John had asked for, they were really upset with them. Jesus called to them, "You all know Romans who use their power to boss and push people around. But that's not the way it is for you. If you want to be great, you must help others. If you want to be first, you must take care of everyone else. I didn't come for people to take care of me. I came to take care of others. I came to give up my life so that many others can live."

Days later they had once more arrived at the old city of Jericho. I, Mark, don't know how long they stayed there. But later Jesus, his disciples, and a crowd of people were on the way out of the city. A blind man, Bartimaeus, was sitting by the roadside begging. His dad's name was Timaeus. When he heard that Jesus was there, he yelled, "Jesus, Son of David, feel sorry for me."

Many people were telling him to be quiet, but he yelled all the more, "Son of David, feel sorry for me."

Jesus stopped and asked them to bring the man to him. They told Bartimaeus, "Have courage! He is asking for you."

The man jumped up, threw down his coat, and the people led him to Jesus. "What do you want me to do for you?" Jesus asked.

The blind man said, "Master, I want to see."

Jesus said, "Go on your way. Because you believed, you are well." Right then the man could see, and he began to follow Jesus on down the road.

Chapter 11

As Jesus and the others were walking to Jerusalem, they came to the villages of Bethphage and Bethany. They were now close to Mount Olive.

Jesus said to two of his disciples, "Go to the village over there. As soon as you get there you'll see a colt tied up that has never been ridden by anyone. Untie it and bring it back here. If anyone asks what you are doing, just say that the Lord needs it. They will let you bring it to me."

They did as he instructed them, and they found the colt outside a house just like he described. While they were untying it, the people standing close by asked, "What are you doing? Why are you untying the colt?"

"Jesus sent us. He told us where we would find this colt," they answered. When the people heard this, they let the disciples take it with them. The disciples brought the colt to Jesus. After they put their coats and sweaters on it like a saddle, he climbed up and sat on it.

As he continued on the road to Jerusalem some people put their garments on the ground in front of Jesus. Others cut down palm branches and spread them out on the road. Those in front of Jesus and those behind him all shouted, "Praise God! Happy is the one who represents the Lord! Blessed is God's Kingdom that is coming for us! Praise God in heaven!"

This is the way Jesus went into Jerusalem. Some even referred to it as a triumphal entry! But Jesus knew what was coming. When he arrived in the city he went immediately into the temple and looked around. Because it was already late, he and his twelve disciples went back to Bethany to spend the night.

The next morning after they left Bethany to go back to Jerusalem, Jesus became hungry. He saw a fig tree in the distance and went to see if it had any fruit on it. When he got to the tree, it only had leaves because it wasn't time for the figs to come out. His disciples were amazed to hear him say to the tree, "May you

never have fruit again."

When they finally got to Jerusalem, Jesus went into the temple. He began throwing out people who were buying and selling things there. He knocked over the tables that were used by the people who collected the money. When the people got up out of their chairs, he knocked over the chairs where they had been sitting to sell doves.

Some people were walking through the temple courtyard so they could get to the market easier. He even stopped them from using the temple as a shortcut to carry their goods to the market.

By now he had everyone's attention, and he began to teach them. He asked, "Doesn't the Old Bible say, 'My house shall be called a house of prayer for everyone?' You have made it a place to rob people!"

The religious leaders heard what Jesus said and began making plans to get rid of him. They were afraid of him because all the people were impressed with his strong teaching.

That evening Jesus and his disciples left the city again. The next morning on the way back to Jerusalem they saw that the fig tree had withered. This reminded them of what had happened the day before. Peter said to Jesus, "Teacher, look! The fig tree which you cursed has withered."

Jesus answered, "Have faith in God. If you believe in God's power, surprising things can happen. You can tell the mountain to be lifted from where it is and be put in the sea. If you believe, it will come true. This is what happens when you pray and ask God to do things. If you believe that you received them from God, your prayers will be answered."

This power of prayer was a new idea to the disciples. They prayed, but they had not realized just how God answered prayer.

Jesus continued his teaching, "And any time you pray, if you are upset about something someone did to you, stop blaming them. Stop feeling angry toward them. If you don't forgive others for what they have done wrong to you, God won't forgive you for what you have done wrong."

When they arrived in Jerusalem again, they went to the temple. While Jesus was walking in the temple, the religious leaders came and asked him, "What right do you have to do what you did yesterday? Who gave you the right to do these things?"

Jesus said, "I will ask you one question. After you answer me, I will tell you by what right I have to do those things. When John baptized, was that from heaven or from men? Answer me."

They talked together, "If we say, 'from heaven,' he will say, 'then why did you not believe him.' If we say, 'from men' . . . hmm."

They were afraid of the crowd. If they answered 'from men' they knew they would be in trouble. The people considered John to be a prophet. So they answered Jesus by saying, "We don't know."

Jesus said to them, "Then I won't tell you by what right I have to do those things."

Chapter 12

❧❧

While he was in the temple, Jesus began to tell parables to the people.

Jesus said, "A man planted a vineyard and built a wall around it. He had a special machine to squeeze the grapes. Underneath the machine the man dug a place for a container to hold the juice. He also built a tower where he could store the juice. He rented the machine and the tower to the farmers who would be taking care of his grapes. Then he left on a trip.

"Eventually the grapes were ripe and ready to pick. The man who had planted the vineyard sent a servant to the farmers. He wanted some of the grapes from his vineyard. The farmers took the servant, beat him, and sent him away without anything."

Some of the young people in the crowd gasped and frowned as if they were feeling the blows.

Jesus kept talking, "Then the man sent another servant. They threw stones and hit him in the head and treated him very mean! The man sent a third servant and this time they killed him."

The tension was increasing among the listeners.

Jesus grew more emphatic, "After that he sent more servants, and they beat some of them and killed others. Eventually he had only one more person to send — his son whom he loved very much. The man thought to himself, 'They will respect my son.' And so he sent his son. But the farmers said, 'This is the one who will inherit everything. Let's kill him. Then we will be able to get the property when the owner dies.' So they killed the son and threw his body out of the vineyard."

The facial expression on many of the listeners showed sorrow and disappointment.

When he had finished the parable, Jesus asked the crowd, "What will the owner of the vineyard do?" Without waiting for a response he continued, "He will come and destroy the farmers and will give the vineyard to others."

Jesus said to them, "Surely you have read what God's Word says! 'The stone the builders did not want to use became the most important stone. This stone came from the Lord and is wonderful to us.'"

The religious leaders knew the scriptures well. Jesus was talking about them in the parable, and they knew it. This certainly made them sure they wanted to capture Jesus and have him killed. But they left him alone and went away because they were afraid of the crowd.

Later they sent some other religious leaders back to Jesus to try to trick him. These leaders asked Jesus, "Teacher, we know you are truthful and don't let other people's ideas change your mind. You just teach God's truth. So tell us, does Caesar, the Roman ruler, have a right to make us pay a tax? Should we pay or not pay?"

Jesus knew they were just pretending that they wanted to know. He asked, "Why are you trying to trick me? Bring a coin for me to see."

They handed one to him, and he looked at it carefully. He handed it back to the man who had given it to him and asked, "Whose picture and name is on this coin?"

They answered, "The Roman Emperor, Caesar's."

Then he said, "Give Caesar the things that belong to Caesar, and give God the things that belong to God." They were amazed at what he said.

Then some other religious leaders, the Sadducees, came to Jesus and began to ask him questions. They did not believe there was life after death.

"Teacher," the spokesman began, "Moses wrote a law that told what was supposed to happen if a married man died and had no children. The law said that his brother is supposed to marry the dead man's wife and have children with her. Let's say that there was a man who had six brothers.

"He married a woman and he died without having any children. The next brother married her, and he died without having children. The next brother married her and he died without having children. The next brother also married her and he died without having any children. Over a period of time, she was married to each brother, and each one died without leaving behind any children.

"Finally, she died too. In the life after death, which brother will be her husband? She's been married to each of them." The group of Sadducees felt rather smug. They thought they had the teacher cornered.

Jesus answered, "Don't you understand God's Word or His power? When people have life after death, they are not married and they don't marry. They are like the angels in heaven."

Since the Sadducees had raised the issue about life after death, Jesus confronted them with this teaching. "Now about the truth that there is life after death — haven't you read what

Moses said in the story about the burning bush? God said, 'I am the God of Abraham and the God of Isaac and the God of Jacob.' He is not the God of the dead, but He is the God of the living. You are wrong to say there is no life after death."

One of the Scribes heard them arguing. He had been listening to the discussion and knew that Jesus had answered the Sadducees very well. He asked him, "What is the most important commandment of all?"

Jesus answered, "Listen, all of you Jews, the Lord our God is one Lord. You shall love the Lord your God with all your heart, and with all your soul, and with all your mind, and with all your strength. The next most important commandment is to love your neighbor as much as you love yourself. There are no commandments that are as great as these."

The Scribe said, "Right, teacher. You have shared the truth that God is the only god. There are no others beside Him. We are to love God with all our heart and with all our mind and with all our strength. And we are to love our neighbor as much as we love ourselves. To do that, indeed, is more important than all of the presents or sacrifices we could give God."

When Jesus heard that the Scribe's answers were so correct, Jesus said, "You are not far from being part of God's Kingdom." After that no one wanted to try asking him any more questions.

As the days passed, Jesus continued teaching in the temple. "Why do the Scribes say that the one called Christ is David's son? With the help of the Spirit of God, David had written, 'The Lord said to my Lord, sit here beside Me until I have given you victory over your enemies.' David calls Him 'Lord,' so how can he be his son?"

No one could answer him.

The crowd enjoyed listening to Jesus. As he taught he said, "Watch out for experts in the Law who like to walk around in long robes. They like to have people give them honor and respect in the market place. They want special seats in the synagogues

and places of importance at banquets.

"They talk to the widows — that's ladies whose husbands have died. They persuade them to give the temple most of their money. The Scribes offer long prayers just so people can see them pray. Some day these people will be in big trouble."

Jesus sat down across from the place where people gave their money to God. He watched how the crowd put money in the offering box and how many rich people put in large amounts. He watched closely as a poor widow came and put in two small coins, which were worth very little.

Jesus turned to his disciples and said, "I say truthfully that this poor widow put in more money than everyone else. They gave their extra money, but even though she was poor, she put in all she owned and all she had."

Chapter 13

ॐ

One day as Jesus was leaving the temple, one of his disciples said to him, "Teacher, look at Jerusalem's beautiful buildings built of such wonderful stones"

Jesus answered, "I want all of you to really get a good look at these great buildings. They will be torn down. Not even one stone will be on top of another one."

The disciples looked at each other. One of the two at the back of the group whispered guardedly, "Do you have any idea what he is talking about?"

His companion shook his head and replied, "I don't have a clue about what he just said." Jesus offered no explanation.

They walked on beyond the gates of the city to Mount Olive. They chose a spot that was directly across the valley from the temple and they sat down there on the mountainside. Some of

them moved away and while no one else was around Peter, James, John, and Andrew began asking questions.

"Jesus, you have been telling us about some events that are going to happen," one mentioned. "Will you tell us when it will be?"

Before he could answer, another asked, "How will we know when all the things have taken place?"

Jesus answered, "Don't let anyone confuse you. Many men will come pretending to be me and will fool a lot of people. When you hear of wars and the threat of wars, don't be afraid. These things must take place, but it is not the end. Countries will fight against countries, and people from one place will fight against people from another place.

"There will be earthquakes in many places, and people will not have the food they need to stay alive. Be very careful. People will make you go to court, and you will be beaten in the synagogues."

"Beaten in the synagogue?" one asked in disbelief.

Jesus nodded, indicating what he said was true. "You will stand in front of governors and kings because of me," Jesus added. "You will have a chance to tell them about me. The Gospel, the good news about God, must be shared in every country. When you are arrested and are put in front of people, don't worry about what you should say. Say whatever you are thinking at that time. The Holy Spirit will be putting the right words in your mind at that very moment."

It was difficult to understand everything he was saying. The four disciples looked at each other and sat silently as Jesus went on talking. They were too shocked to say anything.

"Brothers will be against brothers," Jesus told them. "Fathers will be against children. Children will be against their mothers and fathers. In fact, they will even cause their parents to be killed. Because of me, everyone will hate you. But the person who continues to trust in me will be saved."

There was a shuffling of feet, and you could hear a sigh of relief among the four disciples. That feeling did not last long.

"You will see horrible things standing in the temple," Jesus said. "Those things should not be there because they turn God's holy place into a place of evil. Please understand what I am telling you. When this happens, anyone in the area of Judea should run and hide in the mountains. If anyone is on his housetop, he should come down and leave immediately. He should not go into the house to get anything before he leaves. If anyone is in a field, he should not go back to get his coat. It will be especially bad for mothers who are providing milk to their babies in those days.

"Pray that this won't happen in the winter. This will be the worst time that has ever happened since the beginning when God created everything. It will never be this bad again. The only way anyone will survive is that God will choose to shorten the time. He will do this so the people He chose will be saved."

The disciples just shook their heads.

"If anyone comes to you and says, 'Look, here is the Christ,' or 'Look, there he is,' don't believe them," Jesus cautioned. "People will pretend to be me, and they will act like that they know everything. They will even do miracles to try to make you believe them instead of trusting the truth that you know. Pay attention. I have told you everything before it happens.

"After this worst time is over, the sun will be dark and the moon won't give any light. The stars will be falling from the sky, and the things in the sky will be shaken. Then I, the Son of Man, will come in the clouds. I will have great power and glory. Then I will send out my angels to the whole earth to get all of the people who believed in me."

Jesus paused. The words about his power and glory were comforting to the disciples. This information was a lot for the disciples to understand.

"Now," Jesus was ready to continue, "I want you to learn an important lesson from the fig tree." The disciples smiled. They knew something about fig trees, so it looked like things would get a little easier to understand.

"When its branch becomes soft and the leaves appear, you know that summer is almost here," Jesus reminded them. "I want you to be sure to remember this! When these things that I have talked about happen, you will know that God is close and just about to come. I am telling you the truth. The people in that generation will not die until all of these things have happened. The sky will end and the earth will end, but my words will never end. No one knows the day and time that this will happen.

"It is like a man who went away on a trip. When he left home, he told the people who worked for him to take care of his things. He told each one what they were supposed to do while he was gone. He also told the one who guarded the door to be very watchful.

"So, you be careful and watchful. You don't know when the man of the house will come back from his trip. It might be in the evening, at midnight, or when the rooster crows early in the morning. You don't want him to find you asleep when he gets home.

"Men, I want you to know that it is very important to be very careful!" Jesus ended the lesson.

Chapter 14

It was just two days before the special Jewish holidays called Passover and the Feast of Unleavened Bread. The religious leaders were doing their best to figure out a way to secretly capture Jesus and kill him. "We don't want to do this during the festival because it might cause the people to riot," they said.

In the meantime, Jesus was staying in Bethany at the home of a friend, Simon the leper. While Jesus and others were leaning back in their chairs by the table, an unexpected thing happened. A woman came into the room and she was carrying an expensive bottle containing very costly perfume. Without any explanation she broke the bottle and poured the perfume over Jesus' head.

"Why in the world would you waste that expensive perfume? someone asked in an accusing manner.

"That perfume could have been sold for a lot of money.

That money could have helped a lot of poor people," another added. They were really upset with what the woman had done.

But Jesus said, "Leave her alone. Why do you bother her?  She has done something good for me. There will always be poor people wherever you are, and you can do good things for them any time. But I won't always be here. She has done what she could when she could. She put oil on my body so that it will be ready when I am buried. I am telling you the truth. People will know about what this woman did for me every place the gospel is preached."

When he saw this happen, Judas Iscariot, one of the twelve disciples, made up his mind. He went looking for the most important religious leaders. They were surprised when he approached them. "I know you men have been having a hard time with Jesus," Judas said. "I'm not sure what all you plan to do, but I know you are eager to capture him. Perhaps you could use my help."

The religious leaders were intrigued by his comments and showed their interest by asking, "What do you have in mind?"

"Well," Judas stammered, "I'm on the inside. I know his routine, and I can make it easier for you to get him."

The religious leaders were trying hard not to show their enthusiasm. They glanced around the small group and smiled to each other as they considered what he was willing to do. Finally, one of them overcoming his surprise said to Judas, "That's a great offer." Others nodded in agreement.

"We'll certainly make it worth your while," and they all, including Judas, laughed. "We'll have some money available for you. Keep us informed, and let us know when you are ready."

Judas left the grinning Pharisees and as he walked away alone he began thinking and plotting how he could accomplish what he had just promised. "It will have to be sometime when there is not a crowd around," he thought to himself.

The Festival of Unleavened Bread was always to follow a certain pattern. On the first day of the festival a lamb was to be sacrificed. Then it was roasted and served for dinner as part of the activities of this holiday. At this time the disciples asked Jesus, "Where do you want us to go to prepare the meal?"

He told two of his disciples, "Go into the city. A man who is carrying a pitcher of water will meet you. Follow him to a house and say to the owner, 'The teacher asks where is the room I may use so that I can eat the Passover meal with my disciples?' He will show you a large upstairs room that has supplies and is ready. Make sure everything is in place for us."

The disciples went to the city and found the man just as Jesus had described. They went with the owner to the large upper room, and the two disciples worked hard to prepare the Passover meal. When it was evening, Jesus came there with the rest of his disciples.

While they were sitting at the table, Jesus began talking to them. "I am sharing the truth with you," he said. "One of you eating with me will help the religious leaders capture me."

They became very, very sad. One after another asked, "Am I the one?"

Jesus said, "It is the one of you who will put his hand in the bowl at the same time I do. God's Son will be captured just as God's Word said he would be. It will be terrible for the one who helps the religious leaders capture me. It would have been better for him if he had never been born."

While they were eating, Jesus took bread and prayed for God to make the bread holy. He broke the bread into pieces and gave some to each disciple. Then he said, "Take this and eat it. It will remind you of my body."

Next he took his cup, and after he thanked God for it, he passed it around to the disciples. All of them drank from the cup. Jesus said to them, "This will remind you of my blood - the new promise which is given for the world. I am telling you this truth. I will never take another drink made from grapes until I drink it in the Kingdom of God which is in heaven."

After they sang a song of praise, they left the upper room and walked outside the city to Mount Olive. When they got there, Jesus told them, "You will all run away and hide. God's Word says, 'the shepherd will be killed and all the sheep will be scattered.' But after I am alive again, you will see me in Galilee."

Peter declared, "Even if all the others leave you, I won't. You can count on me!"

But Jesus said to him, "Oh, Peter! The truth is that before you hear the rooster crow twice tonight, you will say you don't know me three times."

Peter said even more strongly, "Even if I have to die with you, Jesus, I will never say I don't know you." The others made similar comments.

As they talked and walked on they came to a beautiful park there on the mountainside. It was called Gethsemane. Jesus said to them, "You have had a big meal and a long walk. Sit here until I have prayed." Then he took Peter, James, and John with him. As they walked on a little farther he became very sad.

He told them, "Inside I am very worried. I have such a deep feeling of danger and sadness that it almost kills me. Stay here and watch."

He left the three disciples and went a little farther and fell on the ground and prayed. He thought if it were possible, he

would not have to go through the events that were about to happen. He prayed, "My dear Father, everything is possible for You. Please help me so I won't have to do this. But I don't want my own way. I want what You want for me." He stayed there a little longer.

Getting up from the ground he went back to the three disciples and found them sleeping. The meal, the walk, the night air, added together making it impossible for them to stay awake. Peter stirred and Jesus said to him, "Simon, are you asleep? Couldn't you stay awake and watch for just an hour? Keep watching and praying so you won't do things that are wrong. I know you really want to do what is right, but you are so weak."

Jesus left them and returned to the place where he had been praying. Again he prayed the same words before going back to the disciples. He found them sleeping the second time. The disciples were disappointed they couldn't stay awake, but they didn't know what to say to him.

Jesus was still troubled and went away for the third time. After praying the same prayer once more, he returned to the disciples. "Are you still resting and sleeping?" he asked. With deep sorrow he said to them, "It is enough. It is now time for me to be turned over to sinners by the disciple who planned this. Let's go to him. He is close to us right now."

Just as he was speaking, Judas and the crowd came toward Jesus. They had been sent by the chief priests and carried swords and clubs with them. Judas had arranged a signal with the leaders of the crowd. "I will kiss the one you want," he said. "Then you can capture him, arrest him, and the guards can take him away."

Judas went immediately to Jesus and said, "Master", and kissed him. As the guards were surrounding him, a person nearby pulled out his sword and hit the slave of the high priest and cut off his ear. Jesus immediately put it back in place with his healing touch.

113

Jesus said to the crowd, "Have you come to get me with swords and clubs as if I were a robber? Every day I was with you in the temple teaching, but you didn't capture me there. But this is happening exactly the way God's Word said it would."

It was a frightening situation. The flickering torches created scary shadows. The crowd looked mean and threatening. Jesus was abandoned by every one of his disciples. They left him there to face the mob alone. A certain young man who had been following Jesus had only one piece of linen clothing wrapped around him. The guards grabbed him, but he wiggled out of the piece of cloth and escaped without any clothes on.

After the betrayal kiss, Jesus was taken directly to the High Priest where all the religious leaders had gathered together. Peter followed them from a distance right into the palace of the High Priest. He sat with the officers and warmed himself by the fire.

The chief priests were trying to find some legal reason for killing Jesus. In fact, the whole council kept trying, but they could not find even one legal reason to do it. Many were lying about him, but they couldn't keep their stories straight. They got events all mixed up.

One man got up and lied as he testified, "We heard him say, 'I will destroy this temple made by men and in three days I will build another one without the help of men.'" Even those things

114

were mixed up, and they were never able to agree among themselves.

Finally, the High Priest go up and came to Jesus and asked him, "Won't you answer and explain what these people are saying about you?" But Jesus kept silent and did not answer.

Then the High Priest asked him, "Are you the Christ, the Son of the Blessed One?"

Jesus answered, "I am. You will see me sitting at the right hand beside God and coming in the clouds of heaven."

Immediately the High Priest tore his own clothes in anger and shouted, "Why do you need to hear anyone else speak? You have heard him say things totally against God. That is blasphemy." Turning to the crowd he asked, "What do you think?"

They all said Jesus deserved to die. Some even spit on him. They blindfolded him and beat him with their fists. Some of the officers slapped his face.

"Tell us what is going to happen in the future," they demanded.

Peter was outside in the yard when one of the servant girls of the High Priest saw him getting warm by the fire. She said to him, "You were with Jesus, the man from Nazareth, too."

But Peter told her, "I don't know or understand what you are talking about." He left the warmth of the fireside and went out to the gate.

Before very long a young woman saw him there and told the people standing around, "This is one of them!" But Peter again said that he wasn't one of them.

After a while, other people standing around said to Peter, "Surely you are one of them because you are from the area of Galilee, too. We can tell by your accent when you speak.

Peter began to speak in anger and hatred, "I don't know this man you are talking about."

Right away the rooster crowed for the second time. Peter remembered how Jesus had said to him, "Before the rooster crows twice, Peter, you will say you don't know me three times."

Peter began to cry.

Chapter 15

❧❦

Early that morning, the chief priests, other leaders, and the whole council met together. They tied Jesus up, took him away and brought him to Pilate, the Roman governor.

When Jesus stood before him, Pilate asked, "Are you the King of the Jews?"

Jesus answered, "What you said is true."

The chief priests accused him of many things. They continued to ask Jesus more questions. Pilate said, "Won't you answer their questions? Did you hear how many bad things they are saying about you?" Jesus did not answer, and Pilate was amazed that Jesus did not talk any more.

Pilate had a custom of letting a prisoner go free each year during the Passover holiday. He always let the crowd choose who he would set free. At this time there was a man, Barabbas, who was in prison for murder. He killed someone when he and some others were fighting against the government.

Leaders of the crowd went to Pilate and asked him to free a prisoner as he usually did at this time. He knew that the religious leaders had captured Jesus because they were jealous of him. He turned to the crowd and asked them, "Do you want me to free the King of the Jews?"

The religious leaders had persuaded the crowd to ask for Barabbas instead of Jesus. When they did, Pilate asked, "What shall I do with this man you call King of the Jews?"

The crowd shouted back, "Crucify him!" Crucifixion is a very painful way to die. To be crucified was to be killed by being nailed to a tree or a cross made of logs or tall boards. The tree or cross was stood upright, and the criminal was left hanging there until he died.

Pilate asked them, "Why? What has he done wrong?"

But the crowd just shouted louder, "Crucify him!"

Because Pilate wanted to please the crowd, he let Barabbas go. After he had Jesus whipped, he ordered his soldiers to crucify him. The soldiers took Jesus into the palace barracks, called the Praetorium, and called other soldiers to join them there.

"Oh, a king must be well dressed," they joked.

"Somebody go get some purple cloth. That's the color for

kings you know," another shouted. So, they covered Jesus' shoulders in the purple cloth looking like a king's robe.

"Every king has to have a crown," they mocked. So they made a crown of thorns and put it on his head. Gathering around him they made fun of him by shouting, "Greetings, King of the Jews!"

They kept hitting his head with a club and spitting on him. They pretended to kneel and bow in front of him. When they got tired of that, they took off the purple robe and put his own clothes back on him. Then they took him out to be crucified.

On the way, they saw a man passing by on his way to the city. It was Simon, the father of Alexander and Rufus. He came from a place called Cyrene on the north coast of Africa. They grabbed him and forced him to carry Jesus' cross. Jesus had fallen because it was so heavy.

They took Jesus to a hill outside of Jerusalem where they executed criminals. It was called Golgotha which meant Place of a Skull. They tried to give him wine mixed with myrrh, a spice they used to prepare people for burial. But he wouldn't drink it.

They nailed him to the cross that he and Simon had carried. Then they raised it into the air and let it drop into the hole which they had dug to stand it in. While he was hanging there on the cross, the soldiers divided up his clothes by throwing dice to decide who got them.

Jesus was crucified at about 9:00 in the morning. The soldiers put a sign on his cross that said, "The King of the Jews." The prophecy from the Old Bible that the Messiah would be treated like a criminal came true. He was crucified with two thieves who were nailed to crosses to die with him.

People passing by on the road into Jerusalem shook their heads and shouted up to Jesus, "Ha! You said you were going to destroy the temple and build it again in three days. Why don't you save yourself and come down off that cross?"

The religious leaders also came by and made fun of Jesus. "He saved others, but now he can't save himself! Why doesn't this Christ, the King and Savior of Israel, come down off the cross? Then we could see and believe him!" they shouted. Even the two robbers hanging beside Jesus made fun of him.

About noon, the whole country became very dark and the darkness lasted until about 3:00 in the afternoon. At that time Jesus yelled out, "Eloi, Eloi, lama sabachthani," which meant,

"My God, My God, why have You forsaken me?"

There were many people standing around where the three crosses were. When they heard it, they said, "He is calling for Elijah!"

A man ran to get a sponge. He put sour wine on it. He used a long stick and offered it to Jesus to drink. They said, "Let's leave him alone and see if Elijah will come to take him down off the cross."

Suddenly Jesus yelled a loud cry and died. At that moment, the long veil in the temple was torn in two all the way from the top to the bottom.

When the soldier who was standing right in front of him saw the way Jesus died, he said, "Truly, this man was the Son of

God!"

Off in the distance away from the crowd there were several women standing and watching. Mary Magdalene, Mary, the mother of James the Less and Joses, and Salome were all there.

They had followed Jesus and served him when he was in Galilee. There were many other men and women who had come up to Jerusalem with him.

Evening came, and it was the day before the Sabbath. Joseph, a man from the town of Arimathea, was an important leader in the religious council. He was a devoted man who was seriously waiting for God's Kingdom. He saw the truth in what Jesus taught. He went boldly to see Pilate with a very special request.

"Pilate," he said, "may I have the body of Jesus? Tomorrow is the Sabbath and I would like to be sure that he is buried before then."

Pilate responded, "Well, it hasn't been very long since the hour of his crucifixion. I wonder if Jesus is even dead yet. Come here, soldier." He called to the soldier who had been standing in front of Jesus at the crucifixion. He asked, "Is it possible that Jesus is already dead?"

"Yes, sir." the soldier replied, "He is dead." Hearing this, Pilate agreed to let Joseph take the body.

Joseph had brought a linen sheet for the burial. He and his servants took the body of Jesus down off of the cross. They wrapped it in linen and laid it in a tomb that had been cut out of a rocky hillside.

Finally, they rolled a stone against the opening to the tomb to seal it closed.

Mary Magdalene and Mary, the mother of Joses, followed them and watched to see where the body of Jesus was laid.

Chapter 16

❧❧

It was two days after the crucifixion and the Sabbath was over! Mary Magdalene, Mary, the mother of James, and Salome went shopping and bought good smelling spices. They purchased the kinds that were used to put on a body to make it ready to be buried. Their plans for placing these spices on the body of Jesus were now complete. They had what they needed.

Early that morning on the first day of the week the three women went to the tomb. In hushed voices they talked together. As they approached the tomb — but before they could see it — one asked, "Who will move the stone for us so we can get into the tomb?" No one had an answer and they continued walking toward the tomb.

Soon they could see the tomb where Jesus had been placed. "Look!" they exclaimed. "The stone has already been moved. The entrance to the tomb is no longer covered. We can go in!" and they hurried forward.

One by one they entered the tomb. Each expressed amazement at what she saw. There, sitting to the right of where

the body of Jesus should have been lying was a young man wearing bright white clothes. He said to them, "Don't be afraid. You are looking for Jesus who was from Nazareth and was crucified. He has come back to life. He is not here. Look, here is the place where they laid him. Go tell his disciples and Peter,

'He is going to Galilee. You will see him there just like he told you.'"

In a state of total astonishment the women rushed out of the tomb. They were frightened, shaking, and totally amazed. They didn't talk to anyone because they were afraid. They left.

Later that day Jesus came to Mary Magdalene and spoke to her. Mary remembered. Several months earlier Jesus had made seven demons leave her. After she had talked with Jesus, she went looking for the disciples. When she found them, it was easy to see that they had been crying and were very sad.

"Oh, I have some wonderful news! Jesus is alive just like he said he would be," Mary told them.

"Mary, what's happened to you? We all know he was crucified," one replied.

Mary answered, "I was at the tomb. James' mother and Salome were there with me. The stone was rolled away, and the tomb was open. All three of us walked right inside. There was a young man there dressed in white who showed us where Jesus had been laid. But the best part was when he told us Jesus is alive." Mary's excitement was *not* contagious. She was extremely disappointed that they did not believe her.

"I don't know what you are talking about, Mary. But we certainly know he died there on the cross," an irritated disciple chimed in. He did not believe her report!

"Listen to me," Mary raised her voice in excitement, "Jesus is alive. I saw him myself. He is alive." No one there was convinced, and Mary Magdalene left the disciples in their misery.

Later Jesus showed up out in the country. Two disciples were walking together — probably sharing their frustrations and disappointments. They met Jesus, but they didn't recognize him

at first. I don't know what happened, but they finally realized who it was. After Jesus talked with them, they went back to share the news with the others.

"You won't believe this, but Mary was right. Jesus is alive. We met him while we were walking through the countryside. He talked with us. It *was* Jesus and *he is alive*." His report was finished and he took a deep breath. The news was *not* believed at all. This group of Jesus' followers were still downhearted.

Another disciple announced his unbelief, "Wait a minute. Not you guys too. Did you forget he was crucified? What's happening to you?"

"Yeah, remember what Joseph did. This man wasn't even one of us, but he went to Pilate and asked for the body of Jesus. Jesus was already dead so Pilate let him have the body," and one more disciple had expressed doubt.

"Well, none of us had nerve enough to do what Joseph from Arimathea did. He had the linen grave cloth and everything else ready, too. We know he took the body of Jesus and placed it in a tomb. Be serious. Dead people don't come back to life on their own." And one more disciple had announced his unbelief.

The two who had seen Jesus spoke almost in unison. "Jesus is alive. You guys know us. Can't you take our word? We saw him! We talked with him. Jesus is alive!" Nothing they said could convince the others that Jesus was alive. The two men who had seen him left, and those they had come to cheer were still sad, distressed, and without hope.

I, Mark, never knew when the next meeting took place. But sometime later when the eleven disciples were all together, Jesus came to them. They were sitting around a table much like they

they did at the Passover meal. And Jesus came! They could scarcely believe it, but there he was. Jesus stood there with them and he was alive.

"Men," Jesus spoke and the chosen eleven listened carefully. "Many days ago I told you what was going to happen. I knew it would be almost impossible for you to understand. Did you hear what I had told you? Didn't you believe me? Did you forget what I had said?

"I met Mary Magdalene the first day of the week. I gave her a message for you. You didn't believe her. Why not? Later I met two of you out walking, and before too long they knew it was me. They came and told you that I am alive. But you still didn't believe it. It made me sad that you did not believe any messenger I sent."

The quiet pause revealed how truly sorry they were that they had not believed the reports. Jesus continued, "My love for you has not changed. There is much work to be done, and I chose you to do it. Here is the assignment I have for you now. Go into all the world and tell everyone about the good news, God loves them. Those who believe and are baptized will be saved. Those who do not believe will be guilty.

"Those who believe will be able to send demons away from people in my name. They will be able to speak in new languages. They will be able to pick up snakes or even drink poison withoutgetting hurt. They will put their hands on sick people, and the people will get well."

After the Lord Jesus finished telling them these things, he went to heaven. He sat down at the right side of God.

The disciples went out everywhere and told everyone about Jesus, and Jesus worked through them. They proved their message was true by the things they did.

This is my story about my friend, Jesus.

The Gospel Storyteller Book Buddy Program

Interested in helping children develop Biblical literacy? Encourage your church to participate in the Gospel Storyteller Book Buddy Program!

It is a one-on-one non-threatening way for tweeners to share their Christian faith by reading the greatest story ever told with a caring adult.

Contact:
Innovative Christian Publications
P.O. Box 20
Grand Haven, Michigan 49417